W9-ATN-206

Laurie Goldman

CLEAN ENERGY

Flash Point

ROARING BROOK PRESS

NEW YORK

Clean
Energy

CONTENTS

[1] ENERGY IN OUR LIVES

Energy is essential. We all need it to stay warm, to cook food, and to light the night.

In the last 200 years, the sources of energy we've grown to depend on most—oil and coal—have transformed the way people live. They've totally changed where we can live and the homes we can live in. They've changed how we travel and how we do business. They've even changed the foods we eat.

So what's the problem? When these fuels burn, they release gases into the air. Some are harmful to people. Others are changing Earth's climate. Two centuries of more and more people burning more and more oil and coal has caused big problems.

It's time to take stock of how much energy we use, what we use it for, and where we get it. And it's time to make choices that are better for our health and kinder to our planet.

A coal-burning power plant in England.

Our Sun's #1

Our *whole planet* is fueled by the Sun. Its energy arrives at Earth in the form of sunlight and provides all of our light and heat. It warms our beaches, drives our weather, and moves water around the planet. And plants capture its energy to make food for the rest of us.

Energy? Who Needs It?

You do! You and every living thing on the planet. Every cell in your body needs energy to function. Your body uses energy to build your bones, move your muscles, pump your blood, digest your food, and even think your thoughts.

Powered by Pasta

Where do you get all that energy? From the food you eat. All that spaghetti, spinach, ice cream, and orange juice is really energy in disguise. It all contains molecules—in the form of carbohydrates, proteins, and fats—that are broken down in chemical reactions to provide fuel for your body. Eat up!

Lighten Up

The Calories in that handful of peanuts? That's a measure of the energy they provide. A Calorie is just a unit of energy. If you eat 2,000 Calories per day, you are using about as much energy as a 100-watt light bulb does in 24 hours. You'd look great in a lampshade.

Nature's Solar Panels

Plants are able to soak up the Sun's energy and use it to make food. They do this in a process called photosynthesis. A plant uses the energy in sunlight to combine carbon dioxide and water into . . . sugar! Bottom line: plants store the Sun's energy in the form of sugars for the rest of us—in tomatoes, potatoes, lettuce, and leaves; in apples, beans, watermelon, and corn. All of us animals on the planet depend on plants to provide fuel—in a digestible form!

Being There

Feel the Burn

Anything you do takes energy. Want to walk to the store? Your muscles burn energy that came from those eggs you ate for breakfast. Don't want to walk? Any form of transportation you choose requires energy. Try streetsailing? The sail catches energy from the wind to blow you down the road. Hop in a car? Its engine burns energy that's stored in the chemical bonds of gasoline—instead of the chemical bonds of food. No, spinach won't work in your car's gas tank.

Good Chemistry

Your body burns fuel—but don't worry, there are no flames involved. A chemical reaction takes place that breaks the bonds that hold the molecules together. The result: two (or more) simpler molecules and the release of . . . energy. The chemical bond was conveniently storing the energy for later use! Very helpful.

You're Getting Warm

As your body burns fuel, it generates heat. That helps keep your internal temperature at a cozy 37°C (98.6°F). But on a cold winter's day, your body needs help keeping you toasty. You might warm your hands over a campfire, or turn on the heat at home. The fuel for the campfire is wood. The fuel that heats your home is probably natural gas. In both cases, the fuel is reacting with oxygen in a chemical reaction that breaks the bonds in the fuel and releases energy as heat. Hot stuff!

Calorie Counter

How much energy did the earliest humans use? Just the energy in the food they ate—about *2,000 Calories a day*. Then they discovered ways to use energy to improve their lives. First, they burned wood to stay warm and to cook their food. Marshmallows would come later. People's energy use jumped to *5,000 Calories a day*. Finally, about 200 years ago, people discovered coal, oil, and natural gas—fossil fuels. Like wood, they can be burned to produce energy. But burning a pound of coal produces a lot more energy than a pound of wood. And a lot more s'mores. Energy use climbed to *80,000 Calories*. What about today? Each of us uses a whopping *230,000 Calories*—if you count everything that makes us comfy—from cars and cell phones to stores filled with our favorite foods and clothes.

Energy-a-Go-Go

Today, energy is used around the world for heat, transportation, electricity, and manufacturing. We use it to light our homes and to keep them warm. We use it to fuel our airplanes and to power our alarm clocks and microwaves. Without energy? We'd be cold, waking up late, and eating raw vegetables in the dark.

WORLD ENERGY USE
About 30% of all the energy the world consumes is for transportation, about 30% is for manufacturing, and, the biggest share, 40% goes into energizing our homes and offices.

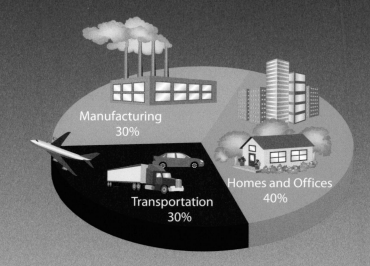

Manufacturing
30%

Homes and Offices
40%

Transportation
30%

Fill 'Er Up

Planes, trains, and automobiles. Yes, people are on the go. But so are the products we use. The food you eat traveled an average of 2,414 kilometers (1,500 miles) to get to your store. That pair of pants made in China? It got here by boat. That lettuce in your salad? A train carried it from central California. That package for Grandma in Iowa? A truck will deliver it to her doorstep. It all takes energy.

I'll Take a Sandwich and a Bottle of Oil

Everything from peanut butter to plastic bottles, from cement sidewalks to cell phones, and from tires to T-shirts takes a lot of energy to make. In fact, more energy goes into manufacturing things and producing food than into anything else.

It takes about 1.5 million barrels of oil a year to make the plastic bottles we chug water from in the U.S.

2

ENERGY TODAY

Where does the world's energy come from today? Over 85 percent of it comes from fossil fuels—coal, oil, and natural gas. The rest comes from a variety of other sources, including wind, water, the nuclei of atoms, and the Sun itself.

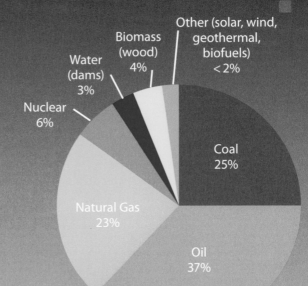

Other (solar, wind, geothermal, biofuels) < 2%

Biomass (wood) 4%

Water (dams) 3%

Nuclear 6%

Coal 25%

Natural Gas 23%

Oil 37%

Being There

What a Crock-Pot!

Fossil fuels? Sounds like dinosaur snack food. That's not far off. These fuels began as plants and animals living in prehistoric oceans and swamps. Over millions of years, their decayed remains were covered by layer after layer of sediment and buried deep within Earth. It was like being in an enormous pressure cooker. The heat and pressure slow-cooked them into the coal, oil, and natural gas we use today. Definitely *not* fast food.

What are fossils fuels used for?

- Most coal is burned in power plants to produce electricity.
- Most oil (95 percent) goes to fuel our transportation.
- Most natural gas is piped into homes for heating and cooking.

How Crude

Our cars burn gas, not oil. Hmm. So somewhere along the way, oil has to be turned into gasoline. The oil that's pumped from underground to the surface is called crude oil—apparently it has no social skills. It's transported through pipelines—sometimes thousands of miles long—to refineries. The refined oil, now called gasoline, is then sent to gas stations, airports, and harbors around the world. And, presumably, its manners have improved.

What a Gas!

Natural gas. Is that gasoline? That would seem logical, but . . . not quite. Natural gas is literally a gas—usually methane, a simple molecule made of one carbon atom and four hydrogen atoms. Most of the natural gas we use is also cooked up over eons, deep within the Earth. It's sent through large pipelines, then smaller ones, until eventually it gets to your home. Turn on the heat? Turn on a burner? You're probably using natural gas.

R U Plugged In?

So how do we get electricity? You can't pump it from a well or dig it out of a mine. And it's not just created behind those outlets in your walls. Electricity is generated from other forms of energy—and just about any kind of energy will do.

Current Events

How does energy go from coal at the power plant to electricity in your home? It's a lot like a giant game of mousetrap. You have to use the energy to do something, which does something else, which does something else . . . .

In many countries, including the U.S., electricity is transmitted to homes and businesses along a complex network of wires called an energy grid. There are three regional grids in the U.S. Which grid are you connected to?

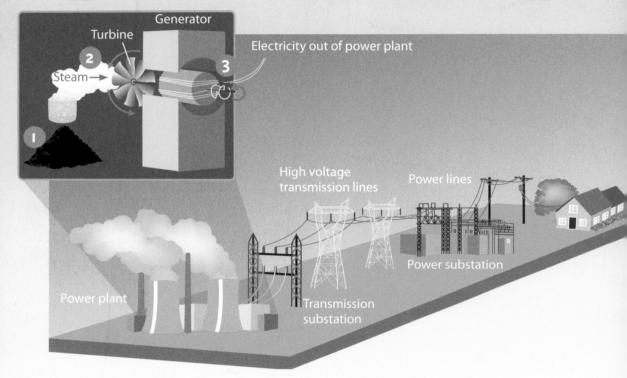

In the U.S, over half of all electricity is generated by burning coal for steam turbines. Here's how it works.

1 Harness the energy in burning coal to heat water to form steam.

2 Direct the steam onto the blades of something that looks like the propeller of an airplane—a turbine. The steam gets the blades spinning. Next, use the mechanical energy of the spinning blades to power a generator. How?

3 Put a set of metal wires on the end of a shaft attached to the turbine. Place it near a magnet. As the turbine blades spin, the shaft spins the wires around in the magnetic field. And that causes the electrons in the wires to start moving. That's an electric current! Now, you've got a generator—a machine that, yes, *generates* electricity.

Go with the Flow

An electric current is just a flow of charged particles—like electrons in a wire. To maintain the current, you have to keep these electrons flowing. So those turbine blades have to keep spinning to power the generator. Many kinds of energy can spin the turbine—wind, water, or steam. You could even spin it by hand—but you wouldn't want to do *that* for too long.

You're a Joule

A joule is a measure of energy. Yes, so is a Calorie. But don't be confused; you can always convert joules to Calories (or vice versa). Why mention joules? Because you're about to encounter—guess watt?

Watt's That?

A what? Yeah, a watt. It's a measure of how much energy—measured in joules—that alarm clock you've got plugged in uses each second. But a watt is not a lot, so it's more common to hear about kilowatts (kW). One kW equals 1,000 watts. Want more watts? A megawatt (MW) is one million of them.

1 watt =1 joule per second

1 kW = 1000 watts = 1000 joules per second

A 10-MW power plant generates 10 million joules of energy per second—enough to power 8,000 homes.

How Much Energy Does it Take?

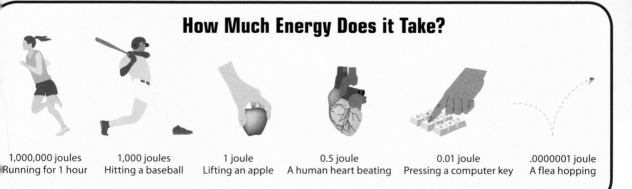

| 1,000,000 joules | 1,000 joules | 1 joule | 0.5 joule | 0.01 joule | .0000001 joule |
| Running for 1 hour | Hitting a baseball | Lifting an apple | A human heart beating | Pressing a computer key | A flea hopping |

3

CHANGING OUR AIR

Why do we choose fossil fuels for so much of our energy? Well, they're definitely habit-forming. They're fairly easy to get and convenient to transport, and we don't have to use them right away. And, at least today, they're one of the cheapest forms of energy. What's *not* to like? Plenty.

Energy, Yes. But . . .

When we burn fossil fuels, we also get the gases and particles that are produced in the chemical reactions that release the energy. These gases drift into the air, and some of them really hurt the environment.

Good Ozone, Bad Ozone

Burning gas in your car releases compounds that react with each other and with sunlight to form ozone. Nothing wrong with that, right? Everyone knows we want ozone in the air to act as our planet's sunscreen and block out ultraviolet (UV) rays before they hit our skin. Yes, but only if we don't have to breathe it! The good ozone is high in the atmosphere, many kilometers above the ground—not low enough to get inhaled into our lungs. Ozone that forms near the ground from gas emitted from tailpipes and smokestacks is chemically the same stuff, but—oh no—it's the major component of smog. It irritates eyes, causes coughing and wheezing, and can even lead to lung damage.

Down and Dirty

Old technology coal-power plants, diesel engines, and industry smokestacks release soot and other microscopic particles into the air. Take a breath of air—you're filling your lungs with more than oxygen. The soot coming out of smokestacks is gunking up lungs around the planet. As a result, more children everywhere are developing asthma and other breathing problems. When you breathe deep, you want it to be clean, fresh air.

Carbonated Planet

Pop open a can of soda, and carbon dioxide bubbles out into the air. Burning fossil fuels also releases carbon dioxide. Lots and lots of it. Scientists have confirmed that the carbon dioxide we've released into the air by burning fossil fuels is affecting Earth's climate. Uh-oh. How's *that* happening?

Our Planet, the Greenhouse

When sunlight strikes the ground, it heats it. The warm ground cools off by radiating heat into the air. Most of the gases in our air, like oxygen and nitrogen, let the heat straight out into space. But certain gases, such as water vapor and carbon dioxide (CO_2), trap some of it before it can escape. Those gases are all present in our atmosphere naturally. And darn good thing too! Without them, Earth's average temperature would be about 33°C (59°F) colder! Even Miami and Los Angeles would be below freezing for most of the year. Brrrrr. Snowy beaches?

2 Much CO$_2$

Once we started burning fossil fuels, we began adding a heap of CO$_2$ into the air. Burning coal adds the most, then oil, then natural gas. All told, we've added 26 billion metric tons! And it doesn't just disappear in the sky. It's up there, and every day more gets added.

Smog over Los Angeles.

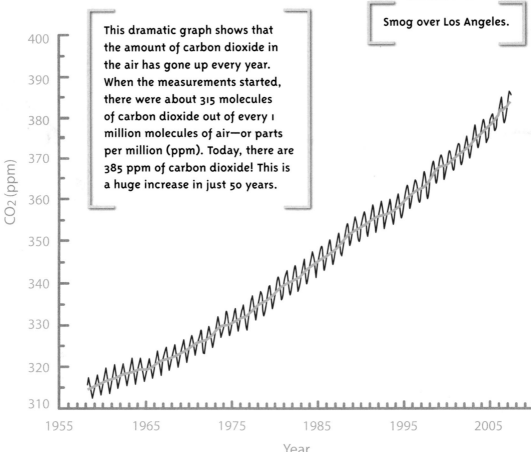

This dramatic graph shows that the amount of carbon dioxide in the air has gone up every year. When the measurements started, there were about 315 molecules of carbon dioxide out of every 1 million molecules of air—or parts per million (ppm). Today, there are 385 ppm of carbon dioxide! This is a huge increase in just 50 years.

Turning Up the Heat

As carbon dioxide builds up, it's adding to the greenhouse effect. And it's warming the planet. Earth's average temperature has risen about 0.8°C (1.5°F) over the last century.

What's the Big Deal?

A degree or two doesn't sound like a lot. But it is. We're already seeing the effects—big time. Arctic sea ice, mountain glaciers, and Antarctic ice sheets are melting—much faster than scientists expected. The oceans are warming. As the warming water expands, sea levels are rising. Weather patterns are changing. Many dry parts of the planet are getting even drier. Rainstorms are more ferocious.

This gushing stream of meltwater on Greenland's ice sheet started as a tiny trickle.

Head for the Hills

Over generations, plants and animals around the world have adapted to conditions in their little part of the planet. Now their homes are changing—and they're on the move. Many are turning up in places that were once too cold for them. Robins are showing up in northern Canada in places where people have never seen them before. Maple trees are packing their trunks and inching north to stay comfortable. Some, unable to adapt to the rapid changes, are in danger of disappearing altogether.

4 U 2 Do

What's Your Carbon Footprint?

If someone asks about your carbon footprint, they're not interested in your shoe size. Your carbon footprint is a measure of the amount of carbon that goes into the air (as CO_2) as a result of all the energy you use. Have your teacher or parent help you find a Web site with a carbon calculator—and use it to determine your own carbon "shoe size."

Hey, Big Foot!

The U.S. and China leave the biggest carbon footprints on the planet. The carbon footprint for the U.S. comes out to the equivalent of about 20 tons of carbon dioxide for each of us, each year. Yikes!

Code Blue Planet

We need energy. But we also need to stop releasing so many pollutants and so much carbon dioxide into the air. That means finding energy solutions that are healthier for ourselves and for our planet. When? Immediately. Is there a doctor in the house?

Passing Gas

Let's see . . . we could use less! That would help immediately. There are lots of ways to conserve energy. Turn lights off when no one's in the room, or buy products with less plastic packaging. Drive less! Here in the U.S., our cars guzzle 60 percent of the energy we use for transportation. That's 150 billion (150,000,000,000!) gallons of gas pumped into our gas tanks each year. Countries where public transportation—trains, buses, light rail—is more popular use much less energy for moving people around. Europe uses half the fuel we do. So hop on your bike—or at least onto a bus!

This parking garage in Amsterdam, the Netherlands, is for bicycles only.

The energy efficient 787 Dreamliner uses 20 percent less fuel than other commercial jets.

Lean Machines

We could use energy more efficiently. That would help right away, too. Engineers are designing much more efficient airplane engines—and some airlines are starting to use them. Modern computers go to sleep when they're not being used. Many new home appliances are much more efficient than the can openers, microwaves, and clothes dryers they'll replace. You can recognize the efficient ones in the store—they'll have an ENERGY STAR rating. Today's refrigerators use 75% less energy than refrigerators built in the late 1970s. Cool!

Clean Up Your Act

And we need to clean up our existing energy sources. Hey, half the world's electricity comes from coal, so let's start there. Old technology coal plants send soot and sulfur dioxide streaming into the air—along with all the carbon dioxide. Those old-style plants are pretty much extinct in the U.S., but they're still being used in many parts of the world. Upgrade those to newer technology—and, by the way, stop building them! In the U.S., soot and pollutants are less of a problem now, but there's even newer technology available to turn the coal to a gas in the coal plant, and then burn the gas. This process pulls out more energy per pound of coal—so less coal is burned to electrify a city, and less carbon dioxide heads into the air.

A bicyclist rides past a coal-burning power plant in Shenyang, China.

Just Bury It

But what if you could catch that carbon dioxide before it gets into the air? Coal gasification techniques are being developed that can do just that. Now, what to do with the carbon dioxide? If it could be buried (sequestered) underground or undersea for thousands of years, that much less carbon dioxide would make its way into the air. Gotcha!

4 U 2 Do

How Green R U?

From the water you use to brush your teeth, to the clothes you wear around the house, to the way you get to soccer practice—do you know how much energy you use? For one week, keep an energy diary. You may be surprised.

Clean Energy World Tour

No matter what we do, we're going to release carbon dioxide when we burn fossil fuels. So we need to find energy sources to replace them—energy sources that are cleaner, and either release much less carbon dioxide or, even better, none at all! There are *lots* of candidates—and people around the world are already using them!

Canada

British Columbia plans to start running one of the first fleets of hydrogen-fueled public buses in 2010. They're building hydrogen fueling stations from Whistler to Victoria.

United States

Kramer Junction, California is the largest solar farm in the world. About the size of New York's Central Park, it makes enough electricity to power 150,000 homes.

Costa Rica

Costa Rica uses a combination of clean energy sources to fulfill most of its electrical needs—wind power, geothermal, and hydroelectric. This new dam (right) will soon be flush with water.

Ireland

The Arklow Bank Wind Farm is off the coast of Ireland. Its seven giant turbines generate enough electricity for 16,000 households.

Iceland

Icelanders get 50 percent of their electricity from geothermal sources. And they heat most of their buildings and hot water with geothermal heat.

China

Soon the entire city of Dontan will run on 100 percent carbon-free energy. Power plants will be fueled with rice husks, wind, and sunlight. And only hydrogen or electric cars will be driven.

France

The La Rance Tidal Power Plant uses the energy in surging tides to power turbines that supply Brittany with four percent of its electricity.

Mali

Biodiesel from local plants helps provide energy to hundreds of African villages that have never had electricity before. The Mali government hopes to eventually supply all 12,000 villages with renewable energy.

[4] HERE COMES THE SUN!

What do the Vatican in Italy, a subway stop in Coney Island (below), and the International Space Station in, uh, space have in common? They all get energy from solar power.

Our 100,000,000,000,000,000-Watt Light Source

Sunlight is a clean, limitless energy source. And, hey, the Sun's going to be around a while— another 4 billion years or so. Any six-year-old knows that if you step into sunlight, you'll get warmer—so adults ought to be able to figure out how to harness it to heat our homes! And for electricity? Its potential is huge. The sunlight hitting Earth in one hour could supply the whole planet's electricity for a year. No carbon dioxide, no pollutants. Now *that's* star power.

Just Soak It Up

Ask any lizard lounging on a warm rock on a cool desert evening— find just the right spot and material, and a little sunshine can go a long way. Architects have learned a lot from lizards. Why not design buildings and homes to take advantage of the sunlight? Orient the windows to let in lots of light, and use stone floors to absorb the heat, and then radiate it back later. But watch out for lounge lizards in the living room.

But How to Bottle Sunlight . . . ?

Any time the Sun heats something, like water, that heat is stored—for a while. The trick is to use the stored heat to generate electricity somehow.

Now Concentrate

How about collecting lots of sunlight with mirrors (left)? Then cleverly focusing all that energy onto pipes carrying oil or water? The intense heat turns the water to steam, the steam turns a turbine, and . . . presto! Just connect that turbine to a generator, and the results are electric!

Tower of Power

No mirrors handy? Build a big glass greenhouse. The Sun heats the air inside. But, hey, hot air rises. So add a tall tower to your greenhouse. Then, as the hot air races up in the tower, have that wind turn the blades of a turbine to generate electricity. Think this is a lot of hot air? There are plans to try it out in Australia.

Photoelectric Fx

Something from Hollywood special effects? Even better—the photoelectric effect enables sunlight to be converted directly to electricity. And it's why solar cells work. Solar cells are made of very thin layers of materials like silicon, a common element found in sand. When sunlight shines on the cell, some of it has enough energy to knock electrons off the silicon atoms and set them free to move around in the cell. Moving charges? Sounds like an electric current. Lights, camera, action!

Being There

Let the Light Shine In!

Kenya has more solar-power systems per person than any other country in the world—more than 30,000 panels are sold there every year. In fact, many remote communities had never had electricity until they installed solar panels.

These women in Nairobi, Kenya are getting ready to bake with sunlight using a solar cook pot. Yum. A Sun-baked cake.

Panel Discussion

A solar panel is made of lots of solar cells. Put several solar panels on a rooftop, and you've got enough electricity for your home; cover a few acres of land with them, and you can power an entire community. Pick a site 200 kilometers (124 miles) square in the sunny western U.S., and you can power the whole country! No joke. What's the catch? You'd need 50 *re-eally* long power cords!

Experts Tell Us

Sarah Kurtz

Solar Cell Scientist
National Renewable Energy Laboratory

Sarah Kurtz develops superefficient solar cells—and they've had some far-out success! They power the Mars rovers. Those rovers were only expected to work for three months, but they surprised everyone, including Sarah. Thanks to her solar cells, the rovers have been rambling around Mars for years.

The idea behind Sarah's supercells? The same as using a magnifying glass to focus sunlight on a piece of paper. Sarah's solar cells concentrate more light with mirrors and lenses. She also captured more of the Sun's energy by designing cells with materials that respond to a wider range of energies in sunlight than traditional solar cells.

Even though her solar cells are already a huge success on another planet, Sarah really prefers working on Earth's rooftops. "It's fun to think that something we invented is running around on Mars," she says. "But the most gratifying thing is that I'm working on the technology that could potentially solve our problems here on Earth."

Spirit (above) and her twin sister, *Opportunity*, are still roving the Martian landscape powered by sunlight.

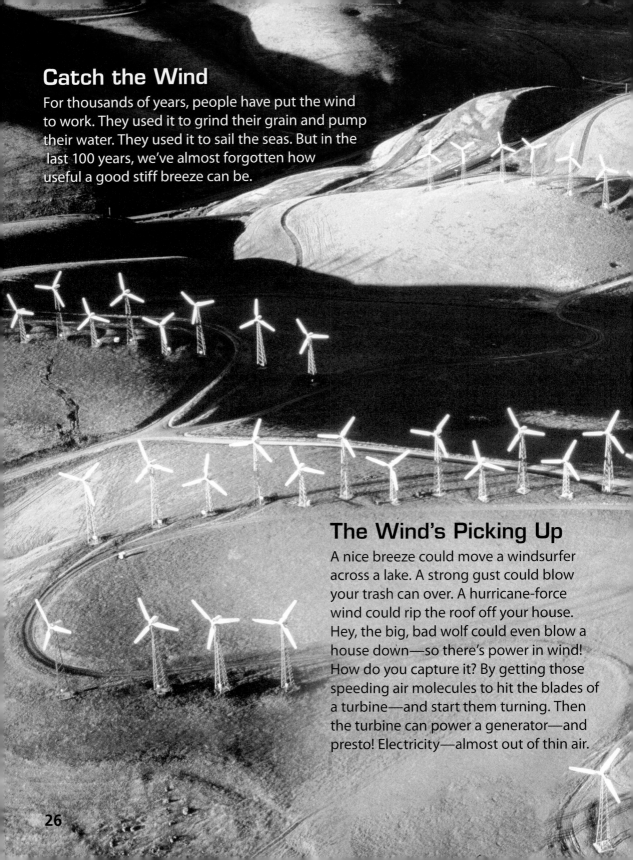

Catch the Wind

For thousands of years, people have put the wind to work. They used it to grind their grain and pump their water. They used it to sail the seas. But in the last 100 years, we've almost forgotten how useful a good stiff breeze can be.

The Wind's Picking Up

A nice breeze could move a windsurfer across a lake. A strong gust could blow your trash can over. A hurricane-force wind could rip the roof off your house. Hey, the big, bad wolf could even blow a house down—so there's power in wind! How do you capture it? By getting those speeding air molecules to hit the blades of a turbine—and start them turning. Then the turbine can power a generator—and presto! Electricity—almost out of thin air.

Wind power generates less than one percent of the world's electricity, but it's the fastest-growing energy source. The image in the background shows a huge wind farm in the hills of Alameda County, California.

The Bigger, the Better

Because air is far less dense than water or even steam, the blades have to be very large so that enough air molecules hit them—and transfer enough energy to them—to get them turning. And it's a good idea to have the turbines high above the ground. There, they'll tap into stronger and more constant breezes. Whoosh.

Go Where the Breezes Blow

Air's everywhere. But wind? Not everywhere. In the U.S., you'd most likely get that windblown look walking along the coast or standing in the vast, flat plains of the Midwest. If you're in Texas, California, or Iowa, hold onto your hat. They are the biggest producers of wind-powered electricity in the U.S.

Being There

Titan Your Turbine

Engineers are designing gigantic turbines to produce huge amounts of energy. These turbines are true titans, with blades longer than a football field, perched atop towers four hundred feet high. Just *one* of these giants can supply energy to more than 1,400 households. That'll blow your socks off.

What Power Light Bulb Are You?

Step 1: Count the Calories you eat in 24 hours.

Step 2: Convert that to joules to get the number of joules of energy you eat (and burn) in 24 hours.

Step 3: How many joules is that per second? (You'll need to know how many seconds there are in 24 hours.)

Wait, that's watts! You burn as much energy in one second as a light bulb of that wattage.

Experts Tell Us

Sally Wright

Mechanical Engineer
Renewable Energy Research Laboratory
University of Massachusetts

After college, Sally Wright designed computer games. But she soon realized that just wasn't for her: "I wanted to do something more meaningful," she remembers. "I liked knowing how things were made, I liked taking things apart—and I wanted to work with energy."

So she went back to school. Now she helps communities develop wind-powered electricity. "I help them decide where to put a wind turbine," she explains. It can take many months just to learn the average wind speed of a site. How much wind is enough? It's got to have an average speed of 23.3 kilometers per hour (14.5 miles per hour)—a moderate breeze— up to 50 meters (164 feet) above the ground. "Wind is variable. People think, 'Oh, you can put wind power anyplace where wind is steady.' Well, there's no such animal!"

Lots of people think Sally has a very cool job. "I talk about my work all the time at parties," she laughs. "Everybody wants to hear about it." But the real benefit? "Every kilowatt hour of energy made by a wind turbine is one that doesn't have to come from fossil fuels."

R. F. Kennedy Elementary School in San Jose, California, has gone green. See the solar panels?

Other Possibilities

Take a look at your school. It probably has a flat roof (nice for solar panels), and it uses most of its electricity during the day. A perfect candidate for solar power? Maybe. What's the average wind speed? Is it a candidate for a wind turbine? Explore the pros and cons of using solar energy or wind power to power your school.

What's the Big Idea?

The potential of solar power is as big as the Sun! But right now it provides less than one percent of the energy we use. What's wrong with this picture?

DOES ENERGY GROW ON TREES?

When we burn fossil fuels, we're getting energy from the Sun that was stored in plants millions and millions of years ago. Thanks, but why wait? We can use plants that aren't so ancient —hey, we can even grow them for fuel. And then we can grow more! If we replant as fast as we cut down, it's even renewable. Even better, the new plants soak in carbon dioxide and help make up for the carbon dioxide released burning the old ones.

A Tree by Any Other Name

…is biomass. It used to go by its low-tech name—wood! For thousands of years it cooked our food, warmed our homes, and illuminated our nights. But as the world's population has grown, that has caused plenty of problems. Forests have been cut down for fuel—and burning wood sends carbon dioxide and lots of polluting smoke into the air. With more than half the world still using wood to cook and to heat their homes, the impact on human health can be devastating.

A mother holds her child as she cooks in her home in Pakistan.

Bionic Biofuels

Today, more modern biofuels supply about three percent of the United State's energy needs. The advantages? Burning them releases less carbon dioxide and fewer pollutants than coal or oil.

Put a Turnip in Your Tank

Biofuels are liquid fuels made from plants. You've heard of ethanol? It's an alcohol, a liquid fuel made from the sugars found in many different plants, including corn, beets, and sugarcane. New technology? I guess not! It was invented in 1826. Early inventor Henry Ford designed his popular Model T to run on either gasoline or ethanol. Beets walking!

How Sweet!

Brazil has taken advantage of its sugarcane crop (right) to become the world's leader in ethanol. More than half the cars in that country now run on some form of it, and using it results in about 50 percent less carbon dioxide released into the air than regular gas. It's working! Brazil has cut its carbon dioxide emissions by 18 percent. Wonder if those cars get a sugar high.

A sugar cane cutter works a plantation in Batatais, Brazil.

It Sounds Corny, But . . .

In the U.S., most ethanol is currently made from corn. But, no joke, there's a problem. It takes energy to turn the starch in those kernels into sugars. That process, which has to occur before the sugar can be fermented to make ethanol, releases . . . carbon dioxide. Whoops. But use the *cornstalks* instead of the *kernels*—then you're really cooking! The cellulose in grasses and stalks is a better choice than starchy corn kernels or grains. How about prairie switchgrass, rice husks, and fast-growing poplar trees? These all grow quicker and use less energy to process into fuel than corn does. Let's save that corn for popping!

Mooo, If You Can Help

Biofuels from cellulose are better—90 percent less carbon dioxide is emitted if these fuels are used instead of gas. But cellulose is a tough customer. The trick is to develop an efficient chemical process for breaking it down to convert it into fuel. So scientists are consulting with the experts . . . cows and termites. They have bacteria living in their guts that help digest the cellulose in wood (for termites) or grass (for cows). The biggest problem? Finding lab coats large enough for Bessy and her friends.

Experts Tell Us

Bryan Willson

Mechanical Engineer
University of Colorado

Bryan Willson has always loved devising new ways to solve old problems. "I invented a great butterfly net when I was five," he remembers. Now his tinkering could help create an efficient biodiesel. Out of what? Algae!

Bryan believes these single-celled plants hold advantages over other biofuel candidates. Algae can convert the sugars they make through photosynthesis into oil. Algae are easy to grow (left), and the *entire* organism is packed with oil, so it's incredibly productive—yielding more oil from a garage-sized patch of land than comes from a football field of soybeans.

But the thing Bryan likes best is that algae can grow in tough conditions. Unlike other biofuels, algae doesn't have to compete against agricultural crops for good land and water. "This shouldn't be a food vs. fuel issue," he explains.

Board the Bio-Bus

Biodiesel, a liquid fuel made from vegetable oils or animal fats, can be used as a carbon dioxide-friendly substitute for regular diesel gas. Most biodiesel today is made from soybeans, but oils from other plants such as coconut and palm are being tried out, too. Biodiesel burns cleaner than fossil-fuel-based diesel or gas, releasing less carbon dioxide into the air. Lots of school districts around the U.S. are converting their buses to biodiesel. Is yours?

Talking Trash

What's that fragrant gas from rotting garbage? It's methane—which can be trapped from dumps and used as an energy source. This biogas can be used for cooking, heating, or powering vehicles. Then there's the commuter train in Sweden (left) running on biogas captured from cow dung and human sewage. Phew!

Gimme a Burger, Fries, and a Fill-up

Do you smell french fries? That car zipping past you might just be a fast-food junkie. Vehicles that use regular diesel can be adapted to run on biodiesel made from FOG—**F**ats, **O**ils, and **G**rease already used by restaurants to fry, say, an order of fries. Make mine to go.

COOL WATER, HOT ROCKS

Just watch a rushing river toss a canoe around. That's water power. People have used it for centuries—and still use it today. Hydropower provides 3 percent of the power used around the world, and over 65 percent of the power used in Latin America and the Caribbean. Good old H_2O.

Use Gravity

There are lots of ways to capture the energy of moving water. A hydroelectric plant uses good old-fashioned gravity to get the job done. Dams are built across rivers in high places, so the water will drop all at once, like a waterfall. The tremendous power of this falling water pushes the blades of—you guessed it—a turbine, which generates electricity. With no carbon dioxide in sight.

¡Gigante!

The Itaipú Dam in South America is gargantuan. To build it, engineers excavated more than 50 million tons of earth and rock and used enough iron and steel to build 380 Eiffel Towers. The hydropower plant at this dam supplies over 75 percent of all the power used in Paraguay and a quarter of that used in Brazil.

The Dam-ages

But dams can still harm the environment. How? They stop rivers in their tracks—and that water needs someplace to wait. Dams form vast lakes or reservoirs, and they can flood ecosystems and sometimes displace people.

Three Gorges is a giant dam across the Yangtze River in China.

Not Enough

Water power is great, but it can't totally solve our energy problems. Even if you could dam up all the rivers on Earth, you couldn't come close to supplying the world's energy needs. So water's a part of the solution, but it will never be the only answer.

Running with the Tide

Wait a minute—water moves in the ocean, too. Ocean currents are invisible rivers of water that never stop flowing. Turbines placed underwater in strong currents, like beneath the Golden Gate Bridge at the entrance to San Francisco Bay, could generate lots of electricity with little environmental impact.

This drawing shows underwater turbines that will soon be built in Ireland near the Irish Sea.

It's Hot Down There!

There's an enormous energy source right under our noses. Well, right under our feet. It's hidden deep inside Earth—we see ferocious evidence of it every time a volcano erupts sending vaporized rock and molten lava into the sky. Geothermal energy starts at the very core of Earth. That's where temperatures, hotter than the surface of the Sun, are sustained by the energy released by the slow decay of radioactive particles. Now, how to harness it?

Geo Whiz!

Dramatic geysers, like Yellowstone's Old Faithful (right), look like steam escaping from an enormous underground teakettle. Superheated water and steam blast straight out of the ground hundreds of feet into the air. Steam piped up from a geothermal source like a geyser can be harnessed to power the blades of a turbine—and generate electricity. Geothermal energy provides way less than one percent of the world's energy. It could definitely contribute more—but it's not the only solution, either.

Direct Heat

In very geologically active lands like Iceland and Japan, people have a very cool way of warming their buildings and water—they pipe hot water from underground reservoirs or hot springs percolating to the surface.

This building in Tokyo, Japan gets 75 percent of its energy from green power, some wind, but mostly geothermal.

Run Out of Steam?

The steam in these geothermal sources can eventually run out. But wait! What about pumping water down there and letting Earth's heat boil it—that would recharge the source. The world's largest geothermal plant, The Geysers of California, is recharged with 42 million liters (11 million gallons) of treated sewage water every day from the city of Santa Rosa, California. Sewage to steam—a good trade.

Hot Rocks

The Earth's heat reserve *is* beneath us everywhere—the trick is reaching down deep enough to retrieve it. Engineers are considering drilling a mile down into layers of hot rock, and then injecting water down to be heated. The hot water and steam would be pumped back up to power turbines. Hot idea!

[7] ENERGY FROM ATOMS

$E = mc^2$

What if you could get enough energy to power a city for a day from a pound of fuel? Well, you can—if the fuel is nuclear fuel. How's that possible? $E=mc^2$, of course.

Gone Fission

There's an enormous amount of energy holding the protons and neutrons together in the nucleus of an atom. If you can "split the atom," you release it—and that process, called nuclear fission, is what's going on inside a nuclear power plant. What atom is being split? A rare but naturally occurring type of uranium. When uranium atoms absorb neutrons, they break into two smaller atoms—releasing more neutrons and *lots* of energy. Where does $E=mc^2$ come in? If you add up the masses of the stuff left after the fission, you'll find that it's less than the mass of the original uranium atom. What happened to that missing mass? Converted to energy! Okay, time to split.

Hi-Tech Teakettle . . .

In a nuclear power plant, the energy that's released is used to heat water for steam-powered turbines that generate electricity. What a way to boil water!

It's All Around

Nuclear power plants already provide about 6 percent of the world's energy—20 percent of the world's electricity! That includes 20 percent of the electricity in the U.S. and nearly 80 percent in France. But there is a problem. Nuclear fission produces a lot of troublesome radioactive waste. Whoops. Better have a really good way to store that used, radioactive material—it's definitely hazardous to your health.

Lots of Bang for the Buck

Nuclear power is mind-boggling—it releases no soot or carbon dioxide into the air, and a little fuel goes a really, really long way. A pound of nuclear fuel provides the same amount of energy as 1,360,777 kilograms (3,000,000 pounds)—a whole trainload—of coal! The problem is the radioactive waste. Solves one problem, creates another. Not insurmountable though. The world just needs some smart engineer to come up with a clever solution . . . how about you?

This nuclear power plant is in northern Germany.

The Hydrogen Generation

Hydrogen is the most common gas in the Universe. It's also the lightest. But it's one heavy-duty fuel source! It rockets the space shuttle off the launch pad, and it is now being used for less spectacular forms of transportation on Earth.

The Space Shuttle *Discovery* roars into the sky toward space.

$2H_2 + O_2 = 2H_2O$ + ENERGY!

When hydrogen gets together with oxygen, the chemical reaction results in energy and . . . water! No CO_2 here. Just good ol' H_2O. Fuel cells are like renewable batteries that use this reaction to create electricity. Hydrogen fuel cells aren't new. They were invented in 1839! Now we're trying to adapt this technology to our current needs.

Hit the Road, Jack

Many experts hope that fuel-cell vehicles will someday help make cars that run on fossil fuels as extinct as the dinosaurs. There are now some cars, trucks, and buses that run on hydrogen fuel cells. The hydrogen is stored as a gas in a special fuel tank. The electricity feeds a battery that powers the vehicle's electric motor. Fill 'er up!

In 2007, there were 160 hydrogen fueling stations worldwide.

So What's the Problem?

Hydrogen may be the most plentiful element in the world, but it rarely travels alone—it's always locked up in molecules with other elements. To get hydrogen for fuel cells, this little element has to be pried from other molecules—often those in fossil fuels, biomass, or water. Unfortunately, this process takes a lot of energy—and releases . . . CO_2. Whoops.

[8] ENERGIZING THE FUTURE

Our world is based on fossil fuels, and we won't change that overnight. But we do need healthier solutions—and we need them quickly.

U Save 5!

There are lots of things we can do right away. Start by using less energy. It helps more than you think. Our energy system is a little like a bucket of water with a hole in the bottom. Energy leaks out all along the way—it takes about 5 joules of energy to get one you can use. So . . . by *not* using a joule, you're actually saving 5! Conserve those joules by turning off gadgets when you don't need them, walking more, and maybe even wearing an extra sweater instead of turning up the heat.

Go Green

Energy-efficient products are hitting the shelves of your local stores. Switch to compact fluorescent lights if you haven't already, buy things with eco-friendly packaging, and look for energy-efficient (ENERGY STAR) electronics.

---

4 U 2 Do

What Do U Think?

Solar. Wind. Biofuel. These are just a few of the cleaner energy sources available. Come up with your own recommendations, using two very scientific tools—research and your own noggin. Start by making a chart of all the alternatives you've learned about with the pros and cons of each. What would you recommend for your home? Your school? Your community?

Make the Switch

But, hey, the most important thing is to switch over to cleaner energy sources. But which ones? Solar, wind, water? There's no silver bullet. Each one has advantages, but each one also has limitations. Solar and wind are squeaky-clean. But it will take time to develop the technologies that will let lots of people use them. Water and geothermal are great, but they can never satisfy all our needs. Biofuels are way better than fossil fuels, but they require energy to process, and they could use up land we need to grow food, if we're not careful.

Way to Go Calgary!

So what's the answer? Just get going! Like Calgary, Canada. Over 75 percent of its electricity comes from wind power. Most of the rest? From biogas trapped from the local landfill. The rail system operates on wind-generated electricity, and city vehicles run on biodiesel.

Working Together

Can we meet our energy challenge? Can we create a more Earth-friendly future? You bet we can!

atmosphere (n.) A layer of gases surrounding a planet or moon, held in place by the force of gravity. (p. 14, 15)

calorie (n.) The amount of heat energy needed to raise the temperature of one gram of water 1°C—also the amount of heat energy that one gram of water releases when it cools down by 1°C. A Calorie (with a capital C) is actually a kilocalorie and is used to indicate the energy content in food. (A kilocalorie is 1,000 calories.) (p. 7, 8, 13, 28)

climate (n.) Prevailing weather conditions for an ecosystem, including temperature, humidity, wind speed, cloud cover, and rainfall. (p. 4, 15)

fossil fuel (n.) Nonrenewable energy resources such as coal, oil, and natural gas that are formed from the compression of plant and animal remains over hundreds of millions of years. (p. 10, 15, 20, 33, 41)

greenhouse effect (n.) The warming that occurs when certain gases (greenhouse gases) are present in a planet's atmosphere. Visible light from the Sun penetrates the atmosphere of a planet and heats the ground. The warmed ground then radiates infrared radiation back toward space. If greenhouse gases are present, they absorb some of that radiation, trapping it and making the planet warmer than it otherwise would be. (p. 16)

greenhouse gases (n.) Gases such as carbon dioxide, water vapor, and methane that absorb infrared radiation. When these gases are present in a planet's atmosphere, they absorb some of the heat trying to escape the planet instead of letting it pass through the atmosphere, resulting in a greenhouse effect. (p. 4, 14, 15)

photosynthesis (n.) Process by which plants use energy from sunlight to convert carbon dioxide and water into food (in the form of sugar). Oxygen is released in the process. (p. 7, 32)